Contents

Contents

1 Prologue: The Spectral Garden
Chapter 1: Owls of the Whispering Woods

The air hung heavy with the scent of damp earth and decaying leaves. Moonlight, fractured by the dense canopy overhead, painted the forest floor in an ethereal mosaic of silver and shadow. This was the whispering woods, a realm where the diurnal world surrendered to the mysteries of the night. Here, the rustling of unseen creatures and the distant hoot of an owl formed a nocturnal symphony, a language whispered between the trees. The spectral garden was alive, pulsating with a hidden energy only perceptible to those who dared to venture into its embrace. This world, veiled in darkness, held secrets waiting to be unveiled, stories whispered on the wind, and a vibrant ecosystem thriving beneath the cloak of night. Within this shadowy realm, the owls reigned supreme, their silent wings carrying them through the moonlit tapestry of branches.

These were the silent hunters, masters of the night, their keen eyesight piercing the darkness with unnerving precision. The Great Horned Owl, with its prominent ear tufts and fierce gaze, perched atop a towering pine, its shadow stretching long across the forest floor. Its deep, resonant hoot echoed through the woods, a territorial call that sent shivers down the spines of smaller creatures. Nearby, a Barred Owl, its haunting call a mournful "Who cooks for you? Who cooks for you?" added a melancholic note to the nocturnal chorus. These owls, with their specialized adaptations, embodied the spirit of the whispering woods, their presence a constant reminder of the hidden power of the night. They were the guardians of the spectral garden, their silent flight a testament to the elegance of nature's design.

The Barn Owl, a ghostly apparition with its heart-shaped face and piercing yellow eyes, glided silently through the open meadow at the edge of the woods. Its specialized hearing allowed it to pinpoint the faintest rustle of a vole hidden beneath the thick grass. These owls, each with their unique hunting strategies and prey preferences, played a vital role in maintaining the delicate balance of the ecosystem. Their presence was not merely a symbol of the night, but an integral part of the intricate web of life that connected every creature within the whispering woods. They were the embodiment of the spectral garden's hidden harmony, their existence interwoven with the fate of the forest itself. Their wisdom, often attributed to their silent observation and nocturnal vigilance, added a layer of mystique to these fascinating creatures.

Their feathers, soft and silent, allowed them to navigate the dense undergrowth without disturbing a leaf, while their powerful talons ensured a swift and decisive kill. The owls were not simply predators; they were a vital part of the forest's intricate balance. They controlled rodent populations, preventing overgrazing and maintaining the health of the understory vegetation. They, in turn, served as prey for larger predators, further solidifying their place in the circle of life. Their existence was a testament to the interconnectedness of all things within the spectral garden, a constant reminder that even the smallest creature played a crucial role in the larger ecosystem. Their silent wings, a symbol of the night, carried with them the weight of ancient wisdom, a knowledge gleaned from generations of nocturnal hunters.

The cultural significance of owls further solidified their place within the spectral garden's mythology. Across cultures, owls have been associated with wisdom, mystery, and magic. Their nocturnal habits and silent flight have often been interpreted as symbols of otherworldly knowledge and a connection to the spirit realm. In some cultures, owls were seen as messengers of the gods, their hoots carrying warnings or prophecies. In others, they were revered as guardians of the night, protecting the world from unseen dangers. These cultural interpretations, woven into the fabric of human history, further enriched the owls' presence within the spectral garden, adding a layer of symbolic meaning to their already fascinating existence. They were not merely birds of prey; they were symbols of the unknown, embodiments of the mysteries that lay hidden within the shadows.

The whispering woods, under the watchful eyes of the owls, held a profound sense of tranquility, a stillness that belied the vibrant life teeming beneath the surface. The owls, with their silent wings and piercing gaze, were the keepers of this stillness, the guardians of the spectral garden's secrets. Their presence, a constant reminder of the hidden wonders of the night, invited us to delve deeper into the mysteries of the whispering woods, to decipher the language of the shadows, and to uncover the secrets of the spectral garden. They were the embodiment of the night, the silent sentinels of the whispering woods, and their story was just one chapter in the larger narrative of the spectral garden.

1.1 Nocturnal Symphony

The forest floor, bathed in the silver glow of moonlight, transforms into a stage. Each rustle of leaves, every snap of a twig, becomes a percussive note in the nocturnal symphony. The hooting of an owl, a mournful yet resonant call, takes center stage, echoing through the trees. This is the realm of the owls, the true conductors of this nighttime orchestra. Their calls, far from random, are complex vocalizations, carrying messages of territorial defense, courtship rituals, and warnings of approaching danger. Each species possesses its unique vocal fingerprint, a distinct dialect in the language of the night. The Great Horned Owl's deep, resonating "hoo-h'HOO-hoo" contrasts sharply with the Barred Owl's more varied and questioning "Who cooks for you? Who cooks for you-all?".

Consider the Eastern Screech-Owl. Its tremulous, high-pitched trill, almost insect-like, belies its fierce predatory nature. This small owl, despite its size, is a formidable hunter, capable of taking down prey larger than itself. From its perch high in the canopy, it listens intently for the slightest rustle in the undergrowth, its large, forward-facing eyes scanning the darkness. The slightest movement triggers a swift and silent descent, talons outstretched, ready to seize its unsuspecting victim. This intricate interplay between predator and prey forms a crucial movement in the nocturnal symphony, a constant push and pull that maintains the delicate balance of the forest ecosystem.

The rustling of leaves, a subtle percussion in this nocturnal orchestra, often signals the movement of small mammals, the primary prey of many owl species. The rustling could be a deer mouse scurrying through the undergrowth, a vole tunneling beneath the leaf litter, or a shrew searching for insects. These small creatures, unaware of the watchful eyes above, play their own unwitting part in the symphony. Their movements, their very existence, fuel the cycle of life and death that sustains the forest.

The wind whispers through the trees, carrying the scent of damp earth and decaying leaves, adding another layer of complexity to the nocturnal symphony. It's a constant, ever-present backdrop to the other sounds of the night, sometimes a gentle breeze, sometimes a powerful gust that shakes the branches and sends leaves swirling to the ground. The wind carries the scent of distant rain, the smell of blooming wildflowers, and the musky odor of nocturnal animals marking their territory. These olfactory cues, invisible yet potent, play a vital role in the communication and navigation of the forest's inhabitants.

As the night progresses, the symphony changes. The hooting of owls becomes less frequent, replaced by the soft, churring calls of nightjars, another group of nocturnal avian musicians. These masters of camouflage, with their mottled brown and grey plumage, blend seamlessly into the shadows. Their calls, a mesmerizing, vibrating churr, add a new dimension to the nocturnal soundscape. These ethereal calls, often lasting for several minutes without pause, are primarily used by males to attract mates and defend their territories. Like the owls, each nightjar species has its own distinct churring pattern, adding another voice to the complex chorus of the night.

The nightjars, unlike the owls, are not perched hunters. They are aerial insectivores, catching their prey on the wing. Their wide mouths and specialized bristles around their beaks help them snag moths, beetles, and other flying insects in mid-air. They patrol the edges of forests and open fields, their silent flight allowing them to approach their prey undetected. Their presence adds another layer of complexity to the predator-prey relationships within the nocturnal ecosystem.

Beneath the forest floor, hidden from view, another, quieter symphony unfolds. The mycorrhizal network, a vast web of fungal filaments, connects the roots of trees and other plants, facilitating the exchange of nutrients and chemical signals. This "wood wide web," as it's often called, plays a crucial role in the health and resilience of the forest ecosystem. While not audible to human ears, this underground network represents a constant hum of activity, a silent exchange of information that sustains the life above.

The mycorrhizal network acts as a conduit for communication between trees, allowing them to share resources and warn each other of impending threats, such as insect infestations or drought. This intricate network of fungal connections highlights the interconnectedness of the forest ecosystem, demonstrating that even seemingly disparate organisms are linked in a complex web of relationships.

The nocturnal symphony, in all its complexity, is a testament to the intricate web of life that thrives under the cover of darkness. From the hooting of owls to the churring of nightjars, from the rustling of leaves to the silent hum of the mycorrhizal network, every sound, every movement, plays a vital role in this grand orchestration of life. By attuning our senses to the subtle nuances of this nocturnal world, we gain a deeper appreciation for the intricate workings of the natural world and the interconnectedness of all living things.

1.2 Silent Hunters

Owls, the quintessential silent hunters, have evolved a suite of remarkable adaptations that allow them to dominate the night. Their predatory prowess stems not from brute strength, but from a refined combination of stealth, exceptional hearing, and specialized vision. Imagine an owl perched atop a towering pine, its feathered form blending seamlessly with the bark. This camouflage, combined with its ability to remain motionless for extended periods, renders it virtually invisible to unsuspecting prey. But the owl's stillness is deceptive. Beneath its feathered cloak, a highly sensitive auditory system is at work.

Asymmetrically placed ear openings, hidden beneath specialized feathers that channel sound, allow owls to pinpoint the location of prey with astonishing accuracy. Even the slightest rustle of a vole scurrying through the undergrowth or the faintest chirp of a cricket hidden beneath a leaf is registered and processed. This auditory acuity is further enhanced by the owl's facial disc, a collection of stiff feathers that acts like a parabolic dish, funneling sound towards the ears. These adaptations allow owls to hunt effectively in complete darkness, relying solely on their hearing to navigate and locate prey.

While their hearing is exceptional, owls' vision is equally remarkable. Their large eyes, fixed in their sockets, provide a wide field of binocular vision, granting them excellent depth perception crucial for judging distances in low light. Unlike many diurnal birds, owls' eyes are packed with rod cells, photoreceptor cells that are highly sensitive to light. This allows them to see in near-darkness, detecting the slightest movement or glimmer of reflected light. However, this specialization comes at a cost. Owls have limited color vision, seeing the world in shades of gray. But in the shadowy realm they inhabit, color is less important than sensitivity to light and movement.

The owl's talons, sharp and powerful, are the final instruments in its hunting arsenal. Once prey is located, the owl launches itself into a silent descent, its wings specially adapted to minimize noise. Soft, downy feathers muffle the sound of air rushing over the wings, allowing the owl to approach its target undetected. Upon reaching its prey, the owl extends its powerful talons, seizing its victim with a swift and deadly grip. The sharp talons pierce the prey, quickly ending the hunt.

Consider the barn owl, a common resident of open fields and farmlands. This species specializes in hunting small rodents, particularly voles, which constitute the bulk of its diet. Barn owls have developed a highly specialized auditory system that allows them to detect the high-pitched squeaks of voles, even amidst the rustling of leaves and the whispering of wind through the grass. This specialized hearing allows them to hunt effectively in dense vegetation, where visual detection is challenging. Their heart-shaped face further enhances their auditory prowess, acting as a sound amplifier.

Contrast this with the Great Horned Owl, a formidable predator that inhabits a wide range of habitats, from forests to deserts. Larger and more powerful than the barn owl, the Great Horned Owl preys on a wider variety of animals, including rabbits, skunks, and even other birds of prey. Their large size and powerful talons equip them to tackle larger prey, while their exceptional night vision allows them to hunt effectively in dimly lit forests. The prominent ear tufts of the Great Horned Owl, often mistaken for ears, are actually just feathers and play no role in hearing. They may, however, serve a communicative purpose, expressing different emotional states.

The silent flight of owls is a testament to their evolutionary refinement. Specialized feathers on the leading edge of their wings break up the airflow, reducing turbulence and minimizing noise. Similarly, the trailing edge of their wings features fringe-like feathers that further dampen sound. This combination of adaptations allows owls to fly almost silently, approaching their prey undetected. Their silent flight contributes to their mystique, adding to the aura of mystery that surrounds these nocturnal hunters.

The ecological role of owls is crucial in maintaining the balance of their respective ecosystems. By controlling populations of rodents and other small mammals, they prevent overgrazing and help maintain the health of plant communities. They also play a role in seed dispersal, indirectly influencing the distribution of plants within their territories. The presence of owls is an indicator of a healthy ecosystem, a testament to the intricate web of life that connects predator and prey. Their silent hunting contributes to the symphony of the night, a subtle reminder of the hidden dramas that unfold under the cover of darkness.

1.3   Wisdom in Feathers

The silent hunter, draped in the twilight hues of the forest, embodies more than just predatory prowess. Owls, with their enigmatic gaze and spectral flight, have long captivated human imagination. Their presence in folklore and mythology transcends mere observation, weaving into the fabric of our cultural understanding of wisdom, mystery, and the unseen world. Consider the Greek goddess Athena, often depicted with an owl perched upon her shoulder, symbolizing wisdom and strategic warfare. This association permeates various cultures, where the owl is seen as a guardian of sacred knowledge, a messenger from the spirit world, or a symbol of profound insight. This deep-rooted connection speaks to the owl's unique place in our collective consciousness, a testament to their captivating aura.

Across diverse cultures, owl symbolism echoes remarkably similar themes. Native American tribes often associate owls with prophecy and protection, believing their calls carry messages from the ancestors. In some African cultures, owls are revered as guardians of the night, their penetrating gaze piercing the veil of darkness to reveal hidden truths. These diverse interpretations underscore a universal fascination with these creatures, a recognition of their connection to the ethereal and the unknown. It's a connection that goes beyond mere superstition, delving into the realm of our inherent fascination with the mysteries of the natural world.

The owl's physical attributes contribute significantly to this mystique. Their forward-facing eyes, unlike most birds, grant them binocular vision, allowing for exceptional depth perception crucial for hunting in low-light conditions. This intense gaze, coupled with their near-silent flight, creates an aura of otherworldly awareness. The specialized feathers, with their serrated edges, muffle the sound of air rushing over their wings, allowing them to approach prey undetected. This mastery of stealth further reinforces their image as silent observers, privy to the secrets whispered in the shadows. Their ability to turn their heads an astonishing 270 degrees enhances this perception, suggesting an all-encompassing awareness of their surroundings.

Beyond their physical adaptations, owls play a vital role in maintaining the delicate balance of their ecosystems. As apex predators, they regulate populations of rodents and other small mammals, contributing to the overall health of the forest. Their presence signifies a thriving ecosystem, one where the intricate web of life remains intact. By studying their hunting patterns and prey selection, we gain valuable insights into the complex dynamics of the forest food web, further enriching our understanding of the interconnectedness of life within these shadowy realms. This understanding highlights the importance of preserving these apex predators, ensuring the continued health and vitality of the forest ecosystem.

Observing owls in their natural habitat provides a profound connection to the natural world. Witnessing their silent flight, hearing the faint rustle of their wings as they glide through the darkness, offers a glimpse into the hidden life of the forest. The soft hooting calls echoing through the trees evoke a sense of mystery and awe, reminding us of the rich tapestry of life that unfolds under the cover of night. By taking the time to appreciate these creatures, we deepen our understanding of the delicate balance that sustains life in the spectral garden. It is a privilege to witness these magnificent birds in their natural element, a reminder of the beauty and complexity of the natural world.

Furthermore, the intricate patterns and subtle coloration of owl feathers offer a visual feast for the discerning eye. The mottled browns, grays, and whites serve as exquisite camouflage, blending seamlessly with the bark of trees and the shadows of the undergrowth. These intricate patterns, unique to each species, are not merely aesthetic; they serve a critical function in the owl's survival. By studying these patterns, we gain insight into the evolutionary pressures that have shaped these creatures over millennia. This appreciation for the beauty and functionality of nature further enhances our connection to the natural world.

Finally, the wisdom often attributed to owls serves as a powerful metaphor for our own journey of self-discovery. Their ability to navigate the darkness, to see beyond the surface of things, reminds us to cultivate our own inner wisdom and to trust our intuition. By embracing the silence and stillness of the night, as the owl does, we can gain access to a deeper understanding of ourselves and the world around us. The owl's quiet observation, its patient vigilance, serves as a reminder of the power of stillness and introspection. It is in these moments of quiet contemplation that we can truly begin to decipher the whispers of the spectral garden.

2 Chapter 2: Nightjars and the Veil of Night

The nightjar, a creature of myth and whisper, embodies the very essence of the veil of night. Its plumage, a masterpiece of camouflage, blends seamlessly with the dusky tapestry of twilight, rendering it virtually invisible to the untrained eye. This mastery of disguise allows the nightjar to become one with the shadows, a phantom flitting through the undergrowth, a whisper on the wind. They are the embodiment of stealth, their presence often only betrayed by their distinctive call, a mechanical churring that resonates through the stillness of the night. This ethereal sound, often described as a sustained, vibrating hum, can vary greatly in pitch and rhythm, adding to the mystique of these elusive birds. The churring can last for minutes at a time, rising and falling, a mesmerizing serenade that echoes through the darkened landscape. These birds are crepuscular and nocturnal hunters, perfectly adapted to a life lived under the cloak of darkness. Their large eyes, specifically designed for low-light conditions, allow them to navigate with ease through the darkest forests and across moonlit meadows. Their wide gapes, fringed with sensitive bristles, act as highly efficient insect nets, snatching moths, beetles, and other flying insects from the air with remarkable precision. This aerial prowess, combined with their silent flight, makes them formidable predators of the night. Their wings, long and pointed, allow for swift, maneuverable flight, enabling them to pursue their prey with remarkable agility.

The nightjar's choice of habitat further underscores its connection to the shadows. They favor open woodlands, heathlands, and forest edges, places where darkness and light intertwine. These transitional zones, known as ecotones, offer a rich tapestry of insect life, providing ample sustenance for these nocturnal hunters. They nest directly on the ground, their mottled eggs blending seamlessly with the leaf litter and bare earth, a testament to their exceptional camouflage. This ground-nesting habit, while making them vulnerable to predators, also reinforces their intimate connection with the earth and the cyclical rhythms of nature. The choice of these specific habitats demonstrates their ability to thrive in diverse environments, adapting to the unique challenges and opportunities presented by each.

The folklore surrounding nightjars is as rich and varied as the landscapes they inhabit. In some cultures, they are associated with witchcraft and ill omens, their nocturnal habits and eerie calls fueling superstitious beliefs. In others, they are seen as benevolent spirits, guardians of the night, their churring calls interpreted as messages from the spirit world. These diverse interpretations highlight the deep impact these enigmatic birds have had on human imagination throughout history. The myths and legends surrounding nightjars reflect the cultural context in which they are perceived, showcasing the complex relationship between humans and the natural world.

Scientifically known as Caprimulgiformes, nightjars are a diverse group of birds found across the globe, with over one hundred different species. They exhibit a remarkable range of adaptations, reflecting the diverse ecosystems they inhabit. From the Common Nighthawk of North America, known for its booming "peent" call and dramatic aerial displays, to the Pennant-winged Nightjar of Australia, with its elongated wing feathers resembling streamers, each species possesses unique characteristics that set it apart. This diversity underscores the adaptability and evolutionary success of these fascinating birds. Studying these variations allows scientists to gain a deeper understanding of the evolutionary pressures that have shaped these remarkable creatures.

The conservation of nightjars and their habitats is crucial for maintaining the delicate balance of the ecosystems they inhabit. Habitat loss due to deforestation, urbanization, and agricultural expansion poses a significant threat to these birds. The use of pesticides also impacts their insect prey, further compounding the challenges they face. Understanding these threats and implementing effective conservation strategies is essential for ensuring the survival of these captivating creatures. Protecting the nightjars means protecting the intricate web of life that supports them, preserving the delicate balance of nature for generations to come. The continued existence of nightjars serves as an indicator of the health of our ecosystems, reminding us of the interconnectedness of all living things.

The churring of the nightjar, a haunting melody echoing through the darkness, serves as a reminder of the hidden wonders that unfold under the veil of night. These masters of twilight, with their cryptic plumage and ethereal calls, embody the mystery and magic of the nocturnal world. By understanding and appreciating these enigmatic birds, we gain a deeper appreciation for the intricate tapestry of life that thrives in the shadows, a world often overlooked and misunderstood. The nightjar, a symbol of the unseen and the unknown, invites us to explore the hidden depths of the natural world, to listen to the whispers of the night and unravel the secrets they hold. Their continued presence in our world enriches our understanding of nature's intricate design, reminding us of the importance of preserving the delicate balance of life on Earth.

2.1   Ethereal Churr

The nightjar's churr is more than just a sound; it's a vibration that permeates the twilight air, a pulsating wave that washes over the listener. This unique vocalization, often described as a sustained mechanical trill, is central to the nightjar's life, serving as a territorial declaration, a mating call, and a crucial element in their nocturnal existence. Unlike the sharp hoots of owls or the melodic songs of diurnal birds, the nightjar's churr is a continuous, almost hypnotic sound, a low thrum that can last for minutes without a break, rising and falling in intensity, sometimes speeding up into a frenzied whir. This continuous, almost otherworldly sound adds to the mystique surrounding these elusive birds, further cementing their place within the tapestry of the nocturnal world. Imagine standing at the edge of a moonlit clearing, the air thick with the scent of damp earth and pine needles, the silence broken only by the rhythmic churring of a nearby nightjar. The sound seems to emanate from the very shadows themselves, a ghostly presence weaving its way through the trees.

The mechanisms behind this remarkable vocalization are equally fascinating. The churr is produced by the male nightjar, primarily during the breeding season. Unlike most birds that vocalize using the syrinx, located at the base of the trachea, the nightjar's churr is thought to be produced by rapid vibrations of the throat muscles and the hyoid apparatus, a complex bone structure that supports the tongue. This unique adaptation allows them to produce the long, sustained trill that characterizes their call. The frequency and pattern of the churr can vary significantly between different nightjar species, adding another layer of complexity to their communication. Some species produce a simple, monotonous churr, while others incorporate intricate variations in pitch and rhythm. These subtle differences allow individual birds to recognize each other and maintain their territories within the complex nocturnal soundscape.

The function of the churr is multifaceted. Primarily, it serves as a territorial signal, broadcasting the male's presence to other males and establishing boundaries within their breeding grounds. The intensity and persistence of the churr can indicate the male's fitness and vigor, making it a key factor in attracting females. During courtship, the male nightjar often performs elaborate aerial displays, accompanied by an intensified churr, creating a mesmerizing spectacle for potential mates. This combination of visual and auditory signals plays a crucial role in mate selection and reinforces the bond between breeding pairs. The churr also serves as a contact call between mates, allowing them to maintain communication in the darkness and coordinate their activities. The subtle variations in the churr can convey information about potential threats or the location of food sources.

Studying the churr offers valuable insights into the complex social dynamics of nightjars. Researchers have discovered that the churr rate, the number of trills per second, can be influenced by various factors, including ambient temperature, moonlight intensity, and the presence of rivals. By analyzing these variations, scientists can gain a deeper understanding of how environmental factors affect nightjar behavior and their reproductive success. The study of nightjar vocalizations also provides crucial information for conservation efforts. By identifying distinct churr patterns, researchers can differentiate between different nightjar species, even in areas where visual identification is challenging. This information is essential for monitoring population trends and assessing the impact of habitat loss and other environmental pressures. Monitoring the changes in churr patterns can provide early warning signs of environmental stress, allowing conservationists to implement proactive measures to protect these fascinating birds and their nocturnal habitats. The churr, therefore, is not merely a sound, but a vital component of the nightjar's survival strategy, a testament to their remarkable adaptation to the shadows, and a window into the hidden language of the night.

2.2 Masters of Twilight

Nightjars, often overlooked denizens of the twilight hours, possess an uncanny mastery of the shadows. Their cryptic plumage, a masterpiece of natural camouflage, renders them virtually invisible against the backdrop of bark, leaf litter, or the dusky earth. This adaptation is paramount to their survival, allowing them to seamlessly melt into their surroundings, whether roosting during the day or lying in wait for unsuspecting prey. Consider the European Nightjar, mottled with shades of grey, brown, and black, effectively disappearing amongst the heather and gorse of its preferred habitat. Or the Pennant-winged Nightjar of Australia, its elongated wing feathers mimicking dried leaves, providing perfect concealment amidst the arid scrublands. This mastery of disguise is not merely a static defense; it's an active component of their hunting strategy.

Their nocturnal habits further solidify their reign over the twilight domain. While diurnal birds retreat to their nests, nightjars awaken, their large, sensitive eyes perfectly adapted to the low-light conditions. These eyes, like polished obsidian, gather every available photon, granting them exceptional vision in the dimness. This visual acuity, coupled with their wide, gaping mouths, fringed with sensitive bristles, transforms them into aerial insectivores par excellence. They become phantoms of the night sky, silently hawking moths, beetles, and other flying insects, their flight paths erratic yet purposeful. The Common Nighthawk of North America, for instance, is known for its dramatic, booming dives, performed during courtship displays or while pursuing prey high above the ground. This aerial acrobatics showcases their agility and control, highlighting their adaptation to a life lived on the wing under the cloak of darkness.

The nightjar's vocalizations are as unique and captivating as their visual adaptations. Their calls, far from the melodious songs of their diurnal counterparts, are often described as churrs, trills, and buzzing hisses. These unusual sounds, produced by specialized vocal cords, carry long distances in the still night air, serving both to attract mates and defend territories. The mysterious "boom" of the Common Nighthawk, created by air rushing through its primary feathers during its steep dives, adds another layer of intrigue to its nocturnal soundscape. These auditory signals, while seemingly simple, represent a complex form of communication, conveying vital information within the darkness. They weave an intricate tapestry of sound, contributing to the unique ambiance of the nocturnal environment.

Beyond their physical adaptations and vocalizations, nightjars exhibit fascinating behavioral patterns that further cement their status as masters of twilight. Their crepuscular activity patterns, peaking during the hours of dawn and dusk, align perfectly with the emergence of their insect prey. This precise timing maximizes their hunting efficiency, allowing them to exploit the abundance of insects drawn to the fading light or the first rays of dawn. Some species, like the Egyptian Nightjar, exhibit a unique form of torpor during periods of cold weather, conserving energy by lowering their body temperature and metabolic rate. This adaptation allows them to survive in harsh environments, demonstrating their resilience and adaptability.

The nesting habits of nightjars are equally remarkable. Eschewing the elaborate nests of many bird species, they opt for simplicity, laying their eggs directly on the ground, often amidst leaf litter or bare earth. This minimalist approach, while seemingly precarious, relies heavily on their exceptional camouflage. The mottled eggs blend seamlessly with their surroundings, rendering them virtually invisible to predators. The parents, equally well-camouflaged, remain vigilant, relying on their cryptic coloration to protect both themselves and their offspring. This intimate connection with the earth, a testament to their mastery of concealment, underscores their deep integration within the nocturnal ecosystem.

Nightjars, in their mastery of twilight, embody the subtle beauty and intricate adaptations of the nocturnal world. Their cryptic plumage, specialized vision, unique vocalizations, and strategic behaviors allow them to thrive in a realm often hidden from human eyes. By understanding these remarkable creatures, we gain a deeper appreciation for the complex tapestry of life that unfolds under the cover of darkness. They remind us that the world of shadows holds just as much wonder and beauty as the sunlit world we know so well. Their presence enriches the nocturnal symphony, adding a layer of mystery and intrigue to the tapestry of life. Their survival strategies, honed over millennia, demonstrate the power of adaptation and the delicate balance that exists within the natural world.

3 Chapter 3: The Mycorrhizal Web: A Hidden Language

Beneath the forest floor, a hidden world thrives. A vast, intricate network of fungal filaments weaves through the soil, connecting the roots of trees and other plants in a complex web of communication and exchange. This is the mycorrhizal network, a symbiotic partnership between fungi and plants that plays a crucial role in the health and stability of forest ecosystems. It's a silent, unseen world, yet its influence is profound, shaping the very fabric of the forest above. This network isn't just a collection of individual threads; it's a dynamic, interconnected system, a living internet of the forest floor.

Mycorrhizae, meaning "fungus root," are formed when fungal hyphae, thread-like structures, colonize the roots of plants. This colonization is not parasitic; instead, it's a mutually beneficial relationship. The fungi extend the reach of the plant's root system, increasing its access to water and essential nutrients, particularly phosphorus and nitrogen. In return, the plant provides the fungi with sugars produced through photosynthesis, a source of energy the fungi cannot produce themselves. This exchange of resources forms the basis of the mycorrhizal symbiosis, a partnership that has been crucial to the evolution and diversification of plants on land. Consider the vast network of tree roots intertwined with fungal hyphae, an intricate dance of give and take beneath the soil surface.

These fungal networks are not simply conduits for resource exchange; they also facilitate communication between plants. Through the mycorrhizal network, plants can share chemical signals, warning each other of impending dangers such as insect attacks or drought. These signals can trigger defensive responses in neighboring plants, allowing them to prepare for the threat and increase their chances of survival. Imagine a network of whispers passing through the soil, a silent language of warning and support. This intricate communication system allows the forest to respond as a unified organism, demonstrating the remarkable interconnectedness of the natural world. The implications of this communication are vast, influencing forest resilience and adaptation to environmental changes.

Different types of mycorrhizal fungi form distinct relationships with plants. Arbuscular mycorrhizae, the most common type, penetrate the root cells of their host plants, forming intricate structures called arbuscules. These arbuscules are the sites of nutrient exchange between the fungus and the plant. Ectomycorrhizae, another prominent type, form a sheath around the root tips of their host plants, creating a network of hyphae that extends into the surrounding soil. Each type of mycorrhiza plays a unique role in the ecosystem, contributing to the overall health and stability of the forest. Understanding the different types helps unravel the complexities of the mycorrhizal world, its intricate relationships shaping the forest's character. The diversity within this hidden world reflects the broader biodiversity of the forest above.

The mycorrhizal web plays a critical role in forest regeneration and resilience. By connecting the roots of seedlings to established trees, the network provides young plants with access to essential resources, increasing their chances of survival. This network also helps to stabilize the soil, preventing erosion and promoting water retention. Furthermore, mycorrhizae enhance the resilience of forests to environmental stresses, such as drought and disease. The fungal network acts as a buffer, helping plants to cope with challenging conditions and recover from disturbances. This interconnectedness fosters resilience in the face of environmental change, ensuring the continuity of the forest ecosystem.

The mycorrhizal network is a testament to the interconnectedness of life in the forest. It highlights the importance of symbiotic relationships and the subtle, yet profound, ways in which organisms interact. By exploring the hidden world beneath our feet, we gain a deeper appreciation for the complexity and beauty of the natural world and the crucial role that fungi play in maintaining the health and stability of our planet's ecosystems. This intricate web of life reminds us that even the smallest, unseen organisms can have a profound impact on the world around us, emphasizing the delicate balance that sustains life on Earth. It underscores the need for a holistic approach to conservation, one that considers the interconnectedness of all living things. The mycorrhizal network, a silent symphony of exchange and communication, remains a crucial component of a healthy, thriving forest.

3.1 Beneath the Surface

The world beneath our feet is a secret realm, a hidden universe bustling with activity. We walk upon it, oblivious to the intricate tapestry of life woven into the very fabric of the soil. This is the realm of the mycorrhizae, a symbiotic partnership between fungi and plants so fundamental to life on land that it's hard to imagine a world without it. Imagine a network of tiny threads, finer than human hair, extending outwards in every direction, connecting the roots of trees and plants in a vast, subterranean web. This is the mycorrhizal network, a hidden highway of information and resources, a silent language spoken between the trees.

This network isn't simply a passive conduit; it's a dynamic and complex system that plays a crucial role in the health and resilience of the entire forest ecosystem. Fungi, through their intricate hyphal networks, extend the reach of plant roots, allowing them to access nutrients and water they couldn't reach on their own. Phosphorus, a vital element for plant growth, is often locked up in the soil, unavailable to plant roots. Mycorrhizal fungi, however, can access and transport this essential nutrient, delivering it directly to the roots of their plant partners. In return, the plants provide the fungi with sugars produced during photosynthesis, a mutually beneficial exchange that fuels life beneath the forest floor.

The benefits of this symbiotic relationship extend far beyond simple nutrient exchange. Mycorrhizal networks act as a communication system, allowing plants to share vital information. When a plant is attacked by insects, it can release chemical signals into the mycorrhizal network, warning nearby plants of the impending danger. These warned plants can then bolster their defenses, preparing themselves for the attack and minimizing the damage. This intricate communication system is a testament to the interconnectedness of life in the forest.

Consider the vastness of these fungal networks. A single teaspoon of healthy soil can contain miles of fungal hyphae. This immense network creates a complex web of interactions, linking plants of different species and allowing them to share resources and information. Older, established trees can use the network to nurture younger seedlings, providing them with essential nutrients and helping them to establish themselves in the competitive environment of the forest floor. This intricate interplay is a key factor in the stability and resilience of forest ecosystems.

The mycorrhizal network isn't simply a conduit for resources; it's a living, breathing ecosystem in its own right. The hyphae of the fungi provide habitat for a diverse community of microorganisms, including bacteria, protozoa, and other fungi. These organisms contribute to the decomposition of organic matter, releasing nutrients back into the soil and further enriching the network. This complex interplay of life beneath the surface highlights the interconnectedness of all living things in the forest.

Furthermore, mycorrhizal fungi play a crucial role in soil structure. Their hyphae bind soil particles together, improving soil aeration and water infiltration. This is particularly important in areas prone to erosion, as the fungal networks help to stabilize the soil and prevent it from being washed away. The intricate network of hyphae acts like a living glue, holding the soil together and maintaining its integrity.

The role of mycorrhizae in carbon sequestration is also becoming increasingly recognized. As plants photosynthesize, they draw carbon dioxide from the atmosphere. A significant portion of this carbon is then transported below ground and stored in the mycorrhizal network, contributing to the long-term storage of carbon in the soil. This makes mycorrhizal networks a crucial component in the global carbon cycle and highlights their importance in mitigating climate change.

The health of the mycorrhizal network is inextricably linked to the health of the entire forest. Disturbances to the soil, such as compaction from heavy machinery or the application of chemical fertilizers, can disrupt the delicate balance of this underground ecosystem. Understanding the vital role of mycorrhizal fungi is essential for responsible forest management and conservation efforts. Protecting this hidden world beneath our feet is crucial for maintaining the health and resilience of our forests and the wider ecosystem. Imagine a forest floor, teeming with life both above and below the surface. The trees, seemingly independent entities, are in fact interconnected through this hidden network, sharing resources, communicating, and supporting each other. This intricate web of life underscores the importance of looking beyond the surface, of recognizing the hidden connections that bind together all living things. The mycorrhizal network is a testament to the power of symbiosis, a reminder that cooperation and interconnectedness are fundamental principles of life on Earth. This hidden world, whispering beneath our feet, is a vital part of the spectral garden, a secret language waiting to be deciphered.

3.2 Fungal Networks

Beneath the forest floor, a vast, intricate network thrives, unseen by the casual observer. This is the realm of the mycorrhizal web, a hidden world of fungal filaments that connect the roots of plants in a complex, symbiotic relationship. Imagine this network as a vast, underground internet, facilitating communication and resource exchange between plants across the forest. This "wood wide web," as it's often called, plays a crucial role in the health and resilience of the entire ecosystem. These fungal threads are not merely passive conduits; they are active participants in a bustling marketplace of nutrients and information.

Mycorrhizae, literally "fungus-root," are formed by the symbiotic association between fungi and plant roots. The fine, hair-like hyphae of the fungi extend the reach of plant root systems, vastly increasing their access to water and essential nutrients like phosphorus and nitrogen. In return, the plants provide the fungi with carbohydrates produced through photosynthesis, a source of energy the fungi cannot produce on their own. This mutually beneficial relationship forms the foundation of a complex underground ecosystem. Think of it as a mutually beneficial trade agreement, where each partner contributes something essential to the other's survival.

Different types of mycorrhizae exist, each with its own unique characteristics and ecological significance. Arbuscular mycorrhizae, the most common type, penetrate the cell walls of plant roots, forming intricate structures called arbuscules. These arbuscules serve as the primary sites of nutrient exchange between the fungus and the plant. Ectomycorrhizae, on the other hand, form a sheath around the root tips, creating a network of hyphae that extend outwards into the soil. This type of mycorrhizae is commonly found in trees, particularly in forests of pine, oak, and birch. Understanding these different types is crucial for appreciating the diverse ways in which mycorrhizal networks influence forest ecosystems.

The mycorrhizal network is more than just a conduit for nutrients; it's a communication highway. Through this network, plants can share vital information about environmental stressors, such as drought or disease. A tree under attack by insects, for example, can release chemical signals through the network, warning its neighbors to bolster their defenses. This inter-plant communication, mediated by the fungal network, contributes significantly to the resilience of the forest community. It allows for a coordinated response to threats, increasing the chances of survival for the entire network.

Furthermore, the mycorrhizal network plays a vital role in seedling establishment. Young seedlings, with their limited root systems, often rely on the established fungal networks to access essential resources. This connection to the wider network can mean the difference between life and death for a young seedling, particularly in harsh environments. The network provides a safety net, ensuring that even the smallest members of the forest community have access to the resources they need to thrive.

The complexity of these fungal networks extends beyond individual plants and even species. Different species of trees can be interconnected through the same mycorrhizal network, facilitating interspecies communication and resource sharing. For instance, a mature tree might provide nutrients to a younger tree of a different species through the network, demonstrating a level of cooperation that transcends traditional ecological boundaries. This interconnectivity highlights the intricate web of life within the forest, showcasing how different species can rely on each other for survival.

However, this delicate underground world is vulnerable to disruption. Soil disturbance, pollution, and unsustainable forestry practices can damage the mycorrhizal network, impacting the health and resilience of the entire forest ecosystem. Understanding the crucial role of these fungal networks is essential for developing sustainable land management practices. Protecting these hidden networks is not just about preserving the fungi themselves, but about safeguarding the interconnectedness of the entire forest.

Consider the implications of this hidden world. The rustling leaves, the hooting owls, the churring nightjars – all are connected by this unseen network beneath the surface. The mycorrhizal web is a testament to the intricate relationships that bind the forest together, a silent symphony of connection and cooperation. Appreciating this hidden language is key to understanding the true complexity and beauty of the natural world. It's a reminder that even in the darkest corners of the forest floor, life thrives in a web of intricate relationships.

Recognizing the significance of these fungal networks is crucial for our understanding and appreciation of forest ecosystems. These hidden threads of connection play a vital role in the health, resilience, and overall functioning of the forest. They are the silent partners in the grand symphony of life, orchestrating the flow of nutrients and information beneath the forest floor. Protecting and preserving these networks is essential for maintaining the health and biodiversity of our forests for generations to come. Their existence is a testament to the intricate web of life, a hidden language whispered between the roots and the soil.

3.3 Whispers in the Soil

The soil beneath our feet is far from inert. It's a vibrant, bustling metropolis of life, a hidden world where an intricate web of interactions takes place. This is the realm of the mycorrhizal network, a symbiotic partnership between fungi and plants that plays a crucial role in the health and resilience of the entire forest ecosystem, particularly impacting the lives of our spectral garden's inhabitants: the owls and nightjars. These fungal filaments, thinner than human hair, weave through the soil, connecting the roots of trees and other plants in a vast underground network.

Think of these fungal networks as nature's internet, a biological communication highway that allows plants to exchange vital nutrients and information. Phosphorus and nitrogen, essential for plant growth, are transported through these fungal pathways, often traveling from areas of abundance to areas of scarcity. This exchange isn't a one-way street; plants reciprocate by providing the fungi with sugars produced through photosynthesis, a vital energy source for the fungi's survival. This intricate exchange allows for a complex communication system, a silent conversation conducted through chemical signals that ripple through the soil. Trees can warn each other of impending insect attacks, sharing chemical defenses that bolster their collective immunity. Seedlings struggling in shaded undergrowth can receive a nutritional boost from larger, established trees through the mycorrhizal network. This intricate web of support fosters a sense of community within the forest, a silent cooperation that underpins the entire ecosystem.

The mycorrhizal network's impact extends beyond mere nutrient exchange; it plays a crucial role in shaping the physical structure of the soil. The fine fungal filaments bind soil particles together, creating stable aggregates that improve soil aeration and water infiltration. This improved soil structure helps prevent erosion and creates a more hospitable environment for a diverse range of soil organisms, from microscopic bacteria to earthworms and insects. This rich soil biodiversity, in turn, supports the growth of a wider variety of plants, creating a more resilient and productive ecosystem. A healthy mycorrhizal network creates a virtuous cycle, promoting soil health, plant diversity, and overall ecosystem stability. This directly affects the abundance of prey species for both owls and nightjars.

Consider the impact on the small mammals, voles and mice, that form a significant part of an owl's diet. These creatures thrive in environments with diverse plant life, nourished by the healthy soils supported by the mycorrhizal network. A robust fungal network leads to a thriving understory, providing ample cover and food sources for these small mammals. This, in turn, supports a healthy owl population, demonstrating the interconnectedness of this subterranean world with the lives of the predators above. Similarly, the abundance of insects, a primary food source for nightjars, is directly linked to the health of the soil and the plants it supports.

The mycorrhizal network, while hidden from view, is a fundamental component of the forest ecosystem. It plays a vital role in nutrient cycling, plant communication, soil structure, and overall ecosystem health. Understanding the intricate workings of this hidden world is crucial to appreciating the delicate balance of the spectral garden. By recognizing the importance of the mycorrhizal network, we gain a deeper understanding of the interconnectedness of all living things within this shadowy realm and the critical role this silent network plays in supporting the lives of the owls and nightjars that grace the night. It's a whisper in the soil, a language understood by the roots of trees, the mycelium of fungi, and, ultimately, the predators that rely on the healthy ecosystem it sustains. This intricate web of life highlights the importance of preserving not just the visible elements of the forest but also the hidden wonders beneath the surface.

The complex interactions within this network are still being unravelled by scientists, who are constantly discovering new complexities and surprising connections. Research suggests that the mycorrhizal network can even influence the composition of plant communities, favoring certain species over others and shaping the overall biodiversity of the forest. The implications of these findings are far-reaching, highlighting the crucial role of fungi in maintaining ecosystem stability and resilience in the face of environmental change. As we delve deeper into the secrets of the mycorrhizal network, we gain a greater appreciation for the intricate web of life that connects all organisms within the spectral garden, a network of whispers that shapes the very foundations of the forest.

This understanding fosters a deeper connection with the natural world, encouraging us to appreciate the hidden beauty and complexity that lies beneath the surface. By acknowledging the vital role of the mycorrhizal network, we gain a greater respect for the delicate balance of the forest ecosystem and the importance of preserving this intricate web of life for generations to come. The whispers in the soil speak volumes about the interconnectedness of nature and the crucial role of these unseen interactions in supporting the life we observe above ground.

3.4 Symbiotic Harmony

The interconnectedness of the forest ecosystem extends far beyond the readily visible interactions between animals and plants. Beneath the soil surface lies a vast, intricate network of fungal filaments known as the mycorrhizal web, a hidden world that plays a crucial role in the health and resilience of the entire forest. This web, formed by the symbiotic relationship between fungi and plant roots, facilitates a complex exchange of nutrients and information, creating a subterranean communication highway that connects trees, shrubs, and other plants in a remarkable way. Think of it as nature's own internet, silently pulsing with life and facilitating the flow of essential resources.

Mycorrhizae, the symbiotic associations between fungi and plant roots, are not a singular entity, but rather a diverse group with varying forms and functions. Arbuscular mycorrhizae, for instance, penetrate the cell walls of plant roots, forming intricate structures called arbuscules within the root cells. These arbuscules serve as the primary sites for nutrient exchange. Ectomycorrhizae, on the other hand, form a sheath around the root tips and grow between root cells, creating a network that extends outwards into the soil. Each type of mycorrhiza plays a specific role in facilitating nutrient uptake and communication within the forest ecosystem.

The fungi in these symbiotic relationships extend their hyphae, thread-like filaments, throughout the soil, creating a vast network that connects the roots of different plants. This network acts as an extension of the plant's root system, increasing its access to water and essential nutrients like phosphorus and nitrogen. In return, the plants provide the fungi with carbohydrates produced through photosynthesis, a mutually beneficial exchange that underscores the interconnectedness of life in the forest. This intricate exchange isn't simply a one-way street; it's a dynamic partnership where both organisms benefit.

Beyond nutrient exchange, the mycorrhizal web also facilitates communication between plants. Through this network, plants can share warning signals about pest attacks or environmental stresses, allowing neighboring plants to bolster their defenses. For example, when a tree is attacked by insects, it can release chemical signals through the mycorrhizal network, alerting nearby trees to the threat. This early warning system allows the neighboring trees to produce defensive compounds, preparing them for the impending attack. This intricate communication system highlights the complex interplay between plants and fungi in the forest ecosystem.

The mycorrhizal web also plays a crucial role in supporting the growth and survival of seedlings. Young trees, often shaded by larger, established trees, have limited access to sunlight and nutrients. The mycorrhizal network can provide these seedlings with the essential resources they need to survive, connecting them to the established trees and allowing them to tap into the established nutrient pathways. This support system is particularly important in dense forests, where competition for resources is intense.

Furthermore, the diversity of fungal species within the mycorrhizal web contributes to the overall stability and resilience of the forest ecosystem. Different fungal species have different strengths and weaknesses, and this diversity creates a buffer against environmental changes and disturbances. A diverse mycorrhizal network can better withstand drought, disease outbreaks, and other challenges, ensuring the continued health of the forest. This resilience is vital for the long-term survival of the forest ecosystem.

The health and complexity of the mycorrhizal network are directly influenced by the overall health of the forest. Practices like clear-cutting, which removes large swathes of trees and disrupts the soil, can severely damage the mycorrhizal network. Similarly, the use of chemical fertilizers and pesticides can also negatively impact the delicate balance of the fungal community. Understanding the importance of this hidden network is crucial for sustainable forest management practices.

Protecting the integrity of the mycorrhizal web is essential for maintaining the health and biodiversity of our forests. By promoting sustainable forestry practices that minimize soil disturbance and avoid the use of harmful chemicals, we can help preserve this vital underground network. Recognizing the interconnectedness of all life within the forest, from the towering trees to the microscopic fungi, is essential for ensuring the continued vitality of these precious ecosystems. The intricate web of life beneath our feet is a testament to the power of symbiosis and the importance of preserving the delicate balance of nature.

The mycorrhizal network plays a critical role in carbon sequestration, the process of capturing and storing atmospheric carbon dioxide. Fungi in the mycorrhizal network contribute significantly to the storage of carbon in the soil, helping to mitigate the effects of climate change. This highlights the importance of preserving these networks in the fight against global warming. Understanding the role of fungi in carbon sequestration is crucial for developing effective climate change mitigation strategies.

Consider the intricate network of hyphae as a vast underground highway system, transporting essential resources and information across the forest floor. This intricate network plays a vital role in maintaining the health and resilience of the forest ecosystem, connecting trees and other plants in a symbiotic relationship. Appreciating the complexity and importance of this hidden world is essential for understanding the interconnectedness of life in the forest.

The mycorrhizal web is a testament to the power of symbiosis in nature, a remarkable example of how different organisms can work together for mutual benefit. By recognizing and protecting this intricate network, we can help ensure the continued health and vitality of our forests for generations to come. This understanding is crucial for fostering a deeper appreciation for the intricate web of life that sustains our planet.

3.5 The Wood Wide Web

Beneath the forest floor, a hidden world thrives. A vast, intricate network of fungal filaments weaves its way through the soil, connecting the roots of trees and other plants in a complex web of communication and cooperation. This is the wood wide web, a biological internet of sorts, where messages are transmitted not through electrical impulses but through chemical signals, nutrient exchanges, and the silent, steady pulse of life itself. This network doesn't just connect individual trees; it binds the entire forest together into a single, interconnected organism. Think of it as the circulatory system of the forest, constantly transporting vital nutrients and information between different parts of the ecosystem.

These fungal filaments, known as hyphae, are incredibly fine, often invisible to the naked eye. They extend outwards from the roots of plants, forming a symbiotic relationship known as mycorrhiza. The fungus receives sugars produced by the plant through photosynthesis, while the plant gains access to a vastly expanded network for absorbing water and nutrients from the soil. This mutually beneficial arrangement is the foundation of the wood wide web, enabling trees and plants to communicate and support one another in remarkable ways. Imagine a single tree struggling to access phosphorus in a nutrient-poor patch of soil. Through the mycorrhizal network, it can connect with a neighboring tree thriving in a richer area and receive the necessary nutrients.

The communication that occurs within the wood wide web isn't limited to simple nutrient exchange. Chemical signals are transmitted through the network, alerting plants to potential dangers. For example, if one tree is attacked by insects, it can release chemical warnings through the mycorrhizal network, prompting nearby trees to bolster their defenses. This early warning system allows the forest to respond collectively to threats, demonstrating a level of cooperation and interconnectedness that is truly remarkable. This fungal network acts as a defense mechanism, allowing the forest to react and adapt to changing conditions.

The wood wide web also plays a crucial role in supporting the growth and development of young seedlings. Established trees, often referred to as "mother trees," can use the network to nurture younger saplings, providing them with essential nutrients and protecting them from the harsh realities of the forest floor. This intergenerational support system ensures the continued health and resilience of the forest ecosystem, allowing new life to flourish under the protective canopy of the old growth. This nurturing aspect of the wood wide web highlights the intricate relationships and dependencies within a forest ecosystem.

The complexity of this underground network is still being unravelled by scientists, but what we know so far is truly astonishing. Different types of fungi form different types of networks, each with its own unique properties and characteristics. Some networks are highly interconnected, while others are more localized. Some specialize in transporting specific nutrients, while others facilitate communication between particular species of plants. This diversity adds another layer of complexity to the wood wide web, creating a dynamic and ever-evolving system of interaction and exchange.

The implications of this interconnectedness are profound. The wood wide web challenges our traditional understanding of forests as collections of individual trees, revealing a deeper level of cooperation and interdependence. It demonstrates the intricate web of life that exists beneath our feet, highlighting the importance of preserving these complex ecosystems. The health of the forest depends not just on the individual trees, but on the health and integrity of the mycorrhizal network that connects them. Understanding this interconnectedness is crucial for developing effective conservation strategies and ensuring the long-term survival of our forests. Consider the impact of deforestation, not just on the trees themselves, but on the intricate network that supports the entire ecosystem.

Furthermore, the discovery of the wood wide web has sparked new avenues of research in fields ranging from agriculture to medicine. Scientists are exploring the potential of harnessing the power of mycorrhizal networks to improve crop yields, enhance plant resilience to drought and disease, and even develop new pharmaceuticals. The intricate communication and resource sharing within these networks offer valuable insights into the complex relationships within ecosystems and provide potential solutions for a variety of challenges. The secrets held within the soil beneath our feet may hold the key to a more sustainable and resilient future.

The exploration of the wood wide web reveals a hidden world of immense complexity and beauty, a world that is essential to the health and survival of our planet. As we continue to unravel the mysteries of this underground network, we gain a deeper appreciation for the interconnectedness of all living things and the vital role that fungi play in maintaining the delicate balance of nature. The wood wide web reminds us that beneath the surface, a silent, intricate conversation is constantly taking place, a conversation that sustains life itself. This is a reminder of the importance of understanding and protecting the hidden wonders of our planet.

4 Chapter 4: Deciphering the Language of Nature

The forest speaks in a language often unheard by human ears. To truly understand the nocturnal world, we must learn to listen with more than just our ears – we must engage all our senses. The rustling of leaves, the snap of a twig, the faintest scent on the breeze—these are the whispers of the forest, each carrying a story. Consider the direction of the wind and how it carries scent; a change in wind direction might signal an approaching predator or a change in weather. Notice the subtle shifts in temperature; a cool pocket of air could indicate a hidden spring or the entrance to a burrow. These seemingly insignificant details become significant when we attune ourselves to the rhythm of the forest.

Learning the language of nature requires patient observation. It's about recognizing patterns and deciphering the subtle cues that reveal the interconnectedness of the ecosystem. Observe the behavior of animals. A flock of birds suddenly taking flight might indicate the presence of a predator, even if you can't see it. Watch how insects interact with plants. The specific plants chosen by certain butterflies for laying their eggs can tell you about the intricate relationships between species. This type of observation, honed over time, provides insights into the complex web of life that unfolds in the shadows.

Think about the way moonlight filters through the canopy, creating patterns on the forest floor. These shifting patterns influence animal behavior, dictating hunting strategies and escape routes. The moon, a silent conductor, orchestrates the nightly ballet of predator and prey. Owls, with their exceptional night vision, use these patterns to their advantage, while their prey seeks refuge in the darkest corners. Observe how the very absence of light plays a role, creating pockets of invisibility and shaping the behavior of creatures adapted to the darkness.

Developing these observational skills is a process of slowing down and immersing oneself in the environment. Find a quiet spot in the forest, preferably during twilight hours. Sit still, breathe deeply, and allow your senses to expand. Start by focusing on one sense at a time. Listen to the sounds around you – the chirping of crickets, the hooting of an owl, the rustle of leaves in the breeze. Close your eyes and try to pinpoint the location of each sound. Then, focus on your sense of smell. What scents can you detect? The damp earth, the decaying leaves, the faint perfume of night-blooming flowers? Try to identify the source of each scent.

As you become more attuned to your surroundings, begin to combine your senses. Notice how the sounds and smells change throughout the evening. How does the temperature shift as the night progresses? What changes in animal activity do you observe? By engaging multiple senses simultaneously, you begin to build a more complete picture of the nocturnal environment. This holistic approach expands our understanding beyond the surface level and reveals the intricate interplay of elements within the forest ecosystem. Document your observations in a journal, sketching what you see and noting the date, time, and weather conditions. Over time, these records will reveal recurring patterns and seasonal changes, deepening your understanding of the forest's rhythms.

Don't be discouraged if you don't see immediate results. Learning to interpret the language of nature takes time and patience. Start with small, manageable goals. Focus on identifying a few common bird calls or learning to recognize the tracks of local mammals. As your knowledge grows, so too will your appreciation for the intricate tapestry of life in the spectral garden. Each new discovery, no matter how small, unlocks a deeper understanding of the natural world. Remember, the forest is a constant source of learning. Even the most experienced naturalists continue to discover new things with each visit. By cultivating a sense of curiosity and a willingness to learn, we can unlock the secrets of the whispering shadows and appreciate the profound beauty of the nocturnal world. The journey of discovery is an ongoing process, a constant unveiling of the intricate language spoken by the natural world. Embrace the challenge and let the forest be your teacher.

4.1   Listening to the Forest

The forest speaks in a multitude of subtle languages, a chorus of rustles, chirps, and whispers that often go unheard by the casual observer. Truly listening to the forest requires more than just hearing these sounds; it demands a conscious effort to attune your senses to the nuances of the natural world, to decipher the intricate interplay of light, shadow, and sound. It's about recognizing patterns and understanding the stories they tell. This isn't simply about identifying bird calls or recognizing animal tracks. It's about immersing yourself in the environment and experiencing the forest as a living, breathing entity.

Begin by finding a quiet spot, preferably at twilight or dawn when the nocturnal and diurnal worlds overlap. Close your eyes and take several deep breaths, focusing on the air filling your lungs, the subtle scents carried on the breeze. Gradually expand your awareness to the sounds around you. The rustling of leaves might indicate a small mammal foraging for food, or perhaps the passage of a larger creature through the undergrowth. The snapping of a twig could signal a deer moving cautiously through the trees.

As you become more attuned to these subtle cues, try to pinpoint the location of each sound. Is it coming from the ground, the understory, or the canopy? Consider the direction of the wind and how it might be carrying sounds from a distance. This practice of directional listening can significantly enhance your ability to interpret the forest's hidden conversations. Imagine, for example, hearing the distant hoot of an owl followed by the alarm calls of smaller birds. This could indicate a hunting owl, revealing a dynamic predator-prey interaction unfolding in real-time.

Beyond sound, observe the interplay of light and shadow. Notice how the dappled sunlight filters through the leaves, creating shifting patterns on the forest floor. These patterns can reveal the movements of insects and the sub-tle changes in the understory vegetation. Observe the way shadows lengthen and deepen as the day progresses, or how moonlight paints the forest in an ethereal glow. These variations in light influence animal behavior, creating distinct shifts in activity throughout the day and night. A clearing bathed in moonlight might become a hunting ground for a nightjar, while the dense shadows beneath a thick canopy might offer refuge to a sleeping rodent.

Another essential element of listening to the forest is understanding the role of scent. The forest floor is rich with olfactory information, from the damp earthiness of decaying leaves to the sweet fragrance of blooming wildflowers. Pay attention to these subtle aromas and how they change with the seasons and weather conditions. The musky scent of a fox might linger on a trail, while the pungent odor of a decomposing carcass could attract scavengers. By incorporating your sense of smell into your observations, you gain a richer understanding of the intricate web of life unfolding around you.

Finally, remember that listening to the forest is a continuous process of learning and discovery. Each visit to the forest offers new opportunities to refine your senses and deepen your understanding of the natural world. Keep a journal to record your observations, noting the date, time, weather conditions, and any significant findings. Over time, these notes will reveal patterns and provide valuable insights into the rhythms and cycles of the forest ecosystem. You'll begin to recognize the distinct calls of different bird species, the subtle signs of animal activity, and the interconnectedness of all living things within the forest. This intimate knowledge will transform your experience of the natural world, allowing you to appreciate the subtle symphony of the forest in a profound and meaningful way. The forest is always speaking; all we need to do is listen.

4.2   Observing the Unseen

The forest floor, a seemingly static landscape of brown and green, holds a hidden world vibrant with activity. Beneath the leaf litter and within the soil, a complex network of life thrives, unseen by the casual observer. This is the realm of the mycorrhizal web, a vast interconnected system of fungal filaments that intertwine with the roots of trees and plants, facilitating a silent exchange of nutrients and information. To understand the nocturnal world, one must learn to perceive this hidden dimension, to look beyond the obvious and grasp the subtle interplay of life beneath the surface.

Developing this awareness requires a shift in perspective, a move away from the purely visual and towards a more holistic sensory experience. The scent of damp earth after a rain, the rustling of leaves in the slightest breeze, the faint snapping of a twig under the weight of a small creature—these are the whispers of the forest, clues to the unseen world. Learning to interpret these subtle cues unlocks a deeper understanding of the intricate relationships that bind the ecosystem together.

Consider the owl, a creature of the night with exceptional hearing. Its asymmetrical ear placement allows for pinpoint accuracy in locating prey hidden beneath the leaves, a testament to the power of auditory perception. By attuning our own ears to the subtle sounds of the forest, we can begin to appreciate the richness of this auditory landscape and glean insights into the activities of its inhabitants. The soft rustle of a vole scurrying through the undergrowth, the barely audible chirping of insects, these sounds paint a picture of the vibrant life that teems beneath the surface.

Beyond sound, the sense of smell also plays a crucial role in deciphering the hidden language of the forest. The musky scent of a fox, the earthy aroma of decaying leaves, the subtle perfume of night-blooming flowers—each scent tells a story, revealing the presence and activities of the forest's inhabitants. By training our noses to discern these subtle olfactory cues, we can gain a richer understanding of the complex chemical communication that takes place within the ecosystem.

The interplay of light and shadow also offers valuable clues. Observe the way moonlight filters through the canopy, casting dappled patterns on the forest floor. Notice how shadows lengthen and shift as the moon traverses the sky. These shifting patterns reveal the contours of the landscape and can highlight the movement of nocturnal creatures, even when they remain hidden from direct view.

Developing this heightened awareness requires patience and practice. Spend time in the forest at different times of day and night, observing the subtle changes in light, sound, and scent. Focus on engaging all your senses, not just your sight. Touch the bark of a tree, feel the texture of the soil, smell the damp leaves. By immersing yourself in the sensory world of the forest, you will begin to perceive the unseen connections that bind the ecosystem together.

The mycorrhizal network, with its vast underground network, exemplifies the interconnectedness of the forest. This hidden web facilitates communication and resource exchange between trees and plants, allowing them to share nutrients and warn each other of impending dangers. Understanding this intricate network allows us to appreciate the complex interdependence of life within the forest.

Think of the nightjar, a master of camouflage that blends seamlessly with the forest floor. Its mottled plumage mimics the dappled patterns of light and shadow, rendering it virtually invisible to predators and prey alike. Observing the nightjar requires keen eyesight and patience, a willingness to slow down and carefully scan the environment. The reward for this effort is a glimpse into the remarkable adaptations that allow creatures to thrive in the shadowy realm of the night.

The ability to observe the unseen is not just a skill; it is a way of connecting with the deeper rhythms of the natural world. By attuning ourselves to the subtle language of the forest, we gain a profound appreciation for the intricate web of life that surrounds us. This awareness deepens our understanding of the ecological processes that shape our planet and fosters a sense of responsibility towards protecting these fragile ecosystems. In the stillness of the night, amidst the whispering shadows, we find a hidden world teeming with life, waiting to be discovered. Through careful observation and a willingness to engage all our senses, we can unlock the secrets of this spectral garden and decipher the language of the unseen.

5 Chapter 5: The Ecology of Shadows

The cloak of night transforms the familiar forest into a realm of secrets. Under the pale moonlight, the hunt begins. An owl, perched high on a gnarled branch, swivels its head, its keen eyesight piercing the darkness. A rustle in the undergrowth, a twitch of a vole's whiskers, and the owl launches into a silent descent, wings barely disturbing the air. This predator-prey relationship, a drama played out nightly, is a cornerstone of the ecology of shadows. The vole, a crucial link in the food chain, sustains not only the owl but also other nocturnal hunters like foxes and weasels. Its existence is intricately woven into the tapestry of the forest floor, where it disperses seeds and aerates the soil, unknowingly contributing to the health of the very plants it consumes.

This delicate balance extends beyond the immediate drama of hunter and hunted. Consider the nightjar, another denizen of the dark. While the owl focuses on small mammals, the nightjar, with its wide gape and specialized bristles around its beak, targets night-flying insects. Moths, drawn to the faint glow of starlight, become unwitting prey. These moths, in their larval stage, may feed on the leaves of trees, contributing to nutrient cycling as their droppings enrich the soil. This intricate web of interactions highlights the interdependence of species within the shadowy ecosystem. Each organism, from the smallest insect to the apex predator, plays a crucial role in maintaining the delicate equilibrium.

Death, too, is an integral part of this cycle. The owl, after consuming its prey, will regurgitate pellets containing indigestible bones and fur. These pellets, scattered on the forest floor, become a valuable source of nutrients for decomposers like fungi and bacteria. These organisms break down the organic matter, releasing essential nutrients back into the soil, nourishing the very trees that support the owl's perch. The mycorrhizal networks, the hidden fungal highways beneath the surface, play a crucial role in this process, transporting nutrients and connecting the roots of trees in a vast, subterranean web. This cycle of life and death, a constant interplay of growth and decay, underscores the interconnectedness of all living things within the ecology of shadows.

The nocturnal world presents unique challenges for its inhabitants. The absence of sunlight limits photosynthesis, forcing plants to adapt in ingenious ways. Some, like the ghostly white Indian pipe, lack chlorophyll entirely and rely on mycorrhizal fungi to obtain nutrients from surrounding trees. Animals, too, have developed remarkable adaptations to survive in the dark. The owl's exceptional hearing allows it to pinpoint the location of prey even in complete darkness. The nightjar's cryptic plumage provides near-perfect camouflage against the backdrop of the forest floor, protecting it from predators and concealing it from unsuspecting prey. These adaptations, honed over millennia of evolution, are testaments to the resilience of life in the face of adversity.

This resilience is further demonstrated by the ability of the ecosystem to recover from disturbances. A fallen tree, for example, creates a gap in the canopy, allowing sunlight to reach the forest floor and triggering a surge of new growth. This, in turn, provides food and shelter for a host of creatures, from insects to deer. The mycorrhizal network plays a crucial role in this recovery process, connecting the roots of surviving trees to the newly established seedlings, facilitating the transfer of nutrients and accelerating the regeneration of the forest. Even in the face of disruption, the ecosystem finds ways to adapt and regenerate, showcasing the inherent resilience of the natural world. This intricate dance of life and death, adaptation and survival, plays out nightly in the spectral garden, a testament to the intricate and resilient nature of the ecology of shadows. The nocturnal world, often shrouded in mystery, reveals its secrets to those who take the time to listen to its whispers and observe its subtle cues. Within the darkness lies a complex and dynamic ecosystem, where every creature, from the smallest microbe to the largest predator, plays a vital role in maintaining the delicate balance of life.

5.1 Predator and Prey

The dance of predator and prey is a ballet of life and death, played out in the hushed theater of the spectral garden. Under the cloak of darkness, the hunter and the hunted engage in an ancient struggle, a drama that shapes the very fabric of the nocturnal ecosystem. Consider the barn owl, a phantom of the night with feathers designed for silent flight. Its acute hearing allows it to pinpoint the rustling of a vole hidden beneath the leaf litter, transforming the smallest sound into a deadly target. This adaptation, honed over millennia, gives the owl a distinct advantage in the darkness, showcasing the intricate link between predator and prey. The vole, in turn, has evolved its own strategies for survival, relying on its keen sense of smell and intricate network of tunnels to evade its aerial nemesis. This constant interplay of adaptation and counter-adaptation drives the evolutionary trajectory of both species, creating a dynamic equilibrium.

The relationship between predator and prey extends beyond a simple hunt. It influences the distribution and abundance of species within the ecosystem. The presence of a predator can regulate the population of its prey, preventing overgrazing or overbrowsing that could damage the delicate balance of the forest. For instance, the presence of owls can help control rodent populations, which in turn affects the health and diversity of plant life. This ripple effect highlights the interconnectedness of all living things within the spectral garden. The removal of a single predator can have cascading consequences, disrupting the intricate web of relationships that sustains the ecosystem.

Consider the nightjar, another denizen of the shadows. This elusive bird, with its cryptic plumage and nocturnal habits, preys on insects drawn to the faint light of the moon. Moths, in particular, form a significant part of the nightjar's diet. These moths, in their larval stage, feed on the leaves of specific trees, contributing to the cycle of nutrient flow within the forest. The nightjar, by controlling moth populations, indirectly influences the health and growth of these trees. This intricate web of interactions underscores the delicate balance that exists within the nocturnal ecosystem. Each species, from the smallest insect to the largest predator, plays a vital role in maintaining the overall health and stability of the spectral garden.

The concept of keystone species further emphasizes the importance of predator-prey relationships. A keystone species, often a top predator, has a disproportionately large impact on its environment relative to its abundance. Its presence influences the structure and function of the entire ecosystem. The removal of a keystone species can trigger a domino effect, leading to significant changes in species composition and ecosystem dynamics. For example, the decline of wolves in certain regions has led to an increase in deer populations, resulting in overbrowsing and a decline in plant diversity. This illustrates the crucial role keystone predators play in regulating their environment.

Even the seemingly silent world beneath our feet, the mycorrhizal network, plays a role in the predator-prey dynamic. These fungal networks, extending like hidden threads through the soil, connect plants in a vast underground web. They facilitate the transfer of nutrients and chemical signals between plants, influencing plant growth and defense mechanisms. A healthy mycorrhizal network can strengthen the defenses of plants against herbivores, indirectly impacting the food sources available to prey animals. This demonstrates the interconnectedness of the entire ecosystem, from the smallest fungi to the largest predators.

The predator-prey relationship is not static but rather a continuous process of adaptation and evolution. As predators develop new hunting strategies, prey evolve new defenses. This ongoing arms race has shaped the incredible diversity of life we see in the spectral garden. Consider the camouflage of certain insects, mimicking the bark of trees to evade detection by birds. Or the evolution of toxins in certain plants, deterring herbivores from consuming them. These adaptations are a testament to the power of natural selection in shaping the intricate relationships between predator and prey.

The study of predator-prey interactions provides invaluable insights into the complexity and resilience of ecosystems. By understanding the intricate web of relationships that connect different species, we can better appreciate the delicate balance of nature and the importance of conservation efforts. Protecting the spectral garden and its inhabitants, from the smallest fungi to the largest predators, is essential for maintaining the health and biodiversity of our planet. The dance of predator and prey continues, a timeless drama that reminds us of the interconnectedness of all living things and the vital role each species plays in the grand symphony of life.

5.2 Balance in the Dark

The cloak of darkness transforms the familiar forest into an alien landscape. Diurnal creatures retreat, and the nocturnal world awakens. This shift isn't merely a change in lighting; it's a fundamental restructuring of the ecosystem's power dynamics. The balance in the dark hinges on a complex interplay of predator and prey, resource availability, and the subtle, often overlooked, influence of the mycorrhizal web. Consider the barn owl, a silent hunter with asymmetrical ears that pinpoint the rustle of a vole in the undergrowth. Its success depends not only on its exceptional hearing, but also on the health of the vole population, which in turn relies on the availability of grasses and forbs, nourished by the unseen fungal networks below. This interconnectedness is the essence of balance.

The mycorrhizal network, that intricate web of fungal filaments weaving through the soil, plays a crucial role in this nocturnal equilibrium. These fungal partners enhance nutrient uptake for plants, including those that provide food and shelter for prey species. A healthy mycorrhizal network contributes to a robust plant community, supporting larger populations of herbivores, which in turn sustain the predators that hunt them. This subterranean network acts as a silent facilitator, a hidden hand orchestrating the flow of energy and resources that underpin the entire nocturnal ecosystem. Without this vital connection, the balance would falter.

Consider the nightjar, a master of camouflage that blends seamlessly with the forest floor. Its cryptic plumage provides protection from predators like foxes and owls, while its wide gape allows it to snatch insects on the wing. This delicate balance between predator avoidance and successful foraging is crucial for the nightjar's survival. Changes in insect populations, driven by factors like climate change or habitat loss, can ripple through the food web, impacting the nightjar and other insectivores. The seemingly simple act of a moth fluttering through the night air is, in fact, a vital thread in the intricate tapestry of the nocturnal ecosystem.

Competition also plays a significant role in maintaining balance. Different owl species, for instance, may specialize in different prey, reducing direct competition. The great horned owl, a formidable predator, might hunt larger prey like rabbits and skunks, while the smaller screech owl focuses on insects and rodents. This partitioning of resources allows multiple predators to coexist within the same habitat. Even seemingly minor variations in prey preference contribute to the overall stability of the nocturnal ecosystem.

Furthermore, the balance in the dark is not static. It is a dynamic process, constantly adjusting to changes in environmental conditions, resource availability, and population fluctuations. A particularly harsh winter, for example, might reduce prey populations, leading to increased competition and potentially even localized extinctions. Conversely, a mild spring could lead to a surge in insect numbers, benefiting insectivores like nightjars and bats. This constant flux is a testament to the resilience of the nocturnal ecosystem, its ability to adapt and reorganize in the face of change.

The concept of "balance" should not be mistaken for harmony. The nocturnal world is a realm of constant struggle, where survival is paramount. Predators and prey are locked in an evolutionary arms race, each adapting to the other's strategies. Owls develop exceptional hearing, while voles evolve heightened senses of smell and touch. This ongoing interplay of adaptation and counter-adaptation drives the evolution of both predator and prey, further refining the intricate balance of the nocturnal ecosystem.

Understanding this intricate balance is crucial for effective conservation efforts. Protecting nocturnal habitats requires not only preserving specific species but also maintaining the complex web of interactions that supports them. Protecting old-growth forests, for instance, provides nesting sites for owls and roosting sites for bats, while also preserving the understory vegetation and the mycorrhizal networks that support their prey. Conservation strategies must consider the entire ecosystem, recognizing that even seemingly small disruptions can have cascading effects.

The darkness hides a complex world of interactions, a silent drama played out under the cloak of night. By understanding the delicate balance of this hidden world, we can better appreciate the intricate tapestry of life that surrounds us, and work to protect its future. The resilience of the nocturnal ecosystem is a testament to the power of adaptation and the interconnectedness of all living things. It's a world where shadows whisper secrets, and the balance of nature hangs in the dark.

5.3 The Cycle of Life

Consider the barn owl, a silent hunter drifting through moonlit meadows. Its prey, the field vole, scurries through the tall grass, unaware of the feathered phantom above. This is a stark illustration of the cycle of life, the constant interplay of predator and prey, life and death, interwoven into the very fabric of the nocturnal ecosystem. The vole, in its turn, consumes seeds and grasses, playing its role in the continuous flow of energy. This seemingly simple act connects it to the earth, the plants, and ultimately, the sun, the original source of energy in this intricate web.

The life cycle of the owl itself is another fascinating layer within this complex tapestry. From the fragile egg nestled within the hollow of an ancient tree, to the fledgling taking its first hesitant flight, to the seasoned hunter ruling its territory, each stage is fraught with peril and opportunity. Survival is a constant challenge, demanding adaptation and resilience. Disease, competition, and changing environmental conditions all play their part in shaping the owl's life, dictating which individuals will successfully reproduce and pass on their genes.

Beneath the surface, a hidden world plays a crucial role in this cycle. The mycorrhizal network, a complex web of fungal filaments, connects the roots of trees and plants, facilitating the exchange of nutrients and chemical signals. This "wood wide web," as it's often called, plays a vital role in the health and resilience of the forest ecosystem, impacting everything from the growth of individual trees to the overall biodiversity of the area. The decay of fallen leaves and other organic matter, facilitated by fungi and other decomposers, releases essential nutrients back into the soil, nourishing the next generation of plants. This process, often overlooked, is a fundamental part of the cycle of life, ensuring the continuation of the forest and all the creatures it supports.

Nightjars, those masters of twilight, also play their part. Their insect-based diet links them to a different set of ecological relationships. The insects they consume, in turn, feed on plants, pollen, and nectar, contributing to pollination and seed dispersal. The nightjar's cryptic plumage and nocturnal habits allow it to exploit a niche where competition is less intense. Their peculiar churring call, echoing through the night, is a testament to their successful adaptation to the shadowy realms they inhabit.

The cycle of life is not simply a linear progression from birth to death. It's a complex, interconnected web, with each organism playing multiple roles. The owl, both predator and prey, contributes to the regulation of prey populations and serves as a food source for other predators. The nightjar, through its feeding habits, influences insect populations and contributes to the health of the plant community. The mycorrhizal network, often unseen, underpins the entire ecosystem, facilitating the flow of nutrients and supporting the growth of the forest.

Think of a fallen tree, a seemingly ending point. Yet, in its decay, it becomes a habitat for insects, fungi, and other organisms, providing sustenance and shelter. This decomposition enriches the soil, providing nutrients for new growth, further demonstrating the cyclical nature of life in the forest. The death of one organism becomes the opportunity for another, a continuous cycle of renewal and transformation.

Consider the seasonal changes within the spectral garden. The abundance of insects in the summer provides ample food for nightjars and their young. The fall brings a bounty of seeds and fruits for the voles, which in turn, become prey for the owls. Winter's harsh conditions test the resilience of all creatures, weeding out the weak and favoring those best adapted to survive. Spring brings rebirth and renewal, a surge of new life as the cycle begins anew.

The intricate relationships between predator and prey, the hidden world of the mycorrhizal network, the adaptations of nocturnal creatures, and the continuous cycle of birth, death, and decay – these are the threads that weave together the rich tapestry of life in the spectral garden. By understanding these intricate connections, we gain a deeper appreciation for the delicate balance of nature and the importance of preserving this fragile ecosystem. Each element, from the smallest insect to the largest owl, plays a crucial role in the ongoing cycle of life, a testament to the interconnectedness and resilience of the natural world.

5.4 Adaptation and Survival

The velvet cloak of night descends, draping the forest in an inky blackness, punctuated only by the faint glimmer of starlight filtering through the canopy. Within this shadowy realm, a silent drama unfolds, a constant struggle for survival where adaptation is not merely an advantage—it's a necessity. Consider the Great Horned Owl, its plumage a masterpiece of camouflage, allowing it to melt seamlessly into the bark of ancient trees. This cryptic coloration, coupled with specialized feathers that muffle the sound of its wings, transforms it into a phantom predator, capable of striking with deadly precision. Its large, forward-facing eyes, designed to gather the faintest glimmers of light, lock onto the slightest movement of a vole scurrying through the underbrush.

Survival in this nocturnal world demands a keen awareness of the environment. The Eastern Screech-Owl, smaller than its horned cousin, relies on a different strategy. Its mottled brown and gray feathers mimic the patterns of tree bark, providing effective concealment during daylight hours. But at night, this small owl becomes a vocal hunter, its piercing trills and whinnies echoing through the darkness, a sonic probe searching for unsuspecting prey. This auditory hunting strategy allows it to locate insects and small mammals hidden beneath leaves or within dense vegetation.

Beyond the feathered hunters, another silent drama plays out beneath the forest floor. The mycorrhizal networks, a vast and intricate web of fungal filaments, connect the roots of trees and other plants in a complex symbiotic relationship. This hidden network facilitates the exchange of nutrients and chemical signals, enabling trees to communicate with one another and support each other in times of stress. During periods of drought, for instance, trees with access to water can share resources with those in drier areas, enhancing the resilience of the entire forest ecosystem. This intricate cooperation underscores the interconnectedness of life within the spectral garden. Consider the nightjar, a master of camouflage and aerial agility. Its mottled plumage, a tapestry of browns, grays, and blacks, blends seamlessly with the leaf litter and fallen branches of the forest floor. This cryptic coloration, combined with its habit of roosting lengthwise along branches, makes it virtually invisible to predators during the day. But as twilight deepens, the nightjar awakens, transforming into an aerial acrobat, its long, pointed wings allowing it to twist and turn with remarkable precision as it snatches insects from the air.

Adaptation also manifests in the unique hunting strategies employed by these nocturnal creatures. The whip-poor-will, a close relative of the nightjar, employs a hawking technique, launching from its perch to capture moths and other flying insects in mid-air. Its wide gape and bristle-lined mouth are perfectly adapted for this feeding strategy, acting like a net to snare its prey. This specialized adaptation allows the whip-poor-will to exploit a food source that is largely unavailable to other nocturnal predators.

The interplay between predator and prey drives the evolutionary dance of adaptation. The long-eared owl, with its asymmetrical ear openings, possesses exceptional hearing, enabling it to pinpoint the faintest rustle of a mouse hidden beneath a blanket of snow. This heightened auditory acuity provides a significant advantage in the dark, allowing the owl to hunt effectively even when visibility is limited. The mouse, in turn, has evolved strategies to avoid detection, relying on its keen sense of smell and its ability to navigate complex burrows to evade its predators.

The ability to adapt to changing environmental conditions is crucial for long-term survival. The Barred Owl, for instance, has demonstrated remarkable adaptability in expanding its range into the territory of the Spotted Owl, a species facing habitat loss and competition. This adaptability stems, in part, from the Barred Owl's broader dietary preferences and its ability to thrive in a wider range of habitats. This adaptability, while beneficial for the Barred Owl, highlights the challenges faced by less adaptable species in the face of environmental change.

The resilience of the nocturnal ecosystem is a testament to the intricate web of life that connects all its inhabitants. From the smallest fungi in the mycorrhizal network to the largest owls perched high in the canopy, each organism plays a vital role in maintaining the delicate balance of this shadowy realm. Understanding these complex interactions is essential for appreciating the beauty and fragility of the spectral garden and for ensuring its continued existence for generations to come. The survival of these species hinges on their capacity to adapt, evolve, and find their niche in the intricate tapestry of the night. Their stories are whispered in the rustle of leaves, the hoot of an owl, and the silent growth of the mycorrhizal web, a constant reminder of the dynamic forces that shape life in the shadows.

5.5 Nature's Resilience

The forest floor, a mosaic of fallen leaves, decaying wood, and emerging shoots, reveals nature's remarkable ability to recover, to regenerate, to persist. Consider the fallen tree, once a towering giant, now a sprawling nurse log. In its decay, it provides a haven for countless organisms: fungi diligently break down its tough fibers, insects burrow into its softening wood, and seedlings find a foothold in the rich compost it creates. This seemingly destructive event fuels a cycle of renewal, fostering life in unexpected ways. The forest doesn't mourn the fallen tree; it embraces the opportunity for transformation.

Disturbances, whether small or large, are an integral part of any ecosystem. A wildfire, though devastating in the short term, can rejuvenate a landscape. It clears out dense underbrush, allowing sunlight to reach the forest floor, triggering the germination of long-dormant seeds. Some tree species, like the ponderosa pine, even require the intense heat of a fire to open their cones and release their seeds. This adaptation ensures their survival and propagation in the face of regular fire cycles. The charred remains become nutrients, enriching the soil for new growth. The resilience of these ecosystems lies in their ability to adapt to, and even utilize, these disruptions.

This capacity for renewal isn't limited to the grand scale of forests and fires. Consider the humble earthworm, tirelessly tunneling through the soil. Its burrowing action aerates the earth, improves drainage, and mixes organic matter with mineral components, creating a fertile environment for plant growth. Even after heavy rains compact the soil, the earthworms, driven by their instinctive behavior, work to restore its structure and porosity, ensuring continued life and growth. Their actions, though small, contribute significantly to the resilience of the soil ecosystem.

The interconnectedness of species within an ecosystem further strengthens its ability to withstand change. The mycorrhizal network, that intricate web of fungal filaments connecting the roots of trees and other plants, plays a vital role in this resilience. This network facilitates the sharing of resources, particularly water and nutrients. During periods of drought, trees with access to water can share this vital resource with less fortunate neighbors through the fungal network, bolstering the overall health and survival of the forest. This cooperative strategy enhances the resilience of the entire ecosystem, allowing it to withstand environmental stresses more effectively.

Predator-prey relationships also contribute to the overall resilience of an ecosystem. While predation might appear detrimental to the individual prey, it plays a crucial role in regulating populations and preventing overgrazing or overbrowsing. Predators often target weaker or diseased individuals, leaving the stronger and healthier members to reproduce and maintain a robust gene pool. This natural selection process strengthens the prey population over time, making it more resilient to disease and environmental changes. This intricate dance of life and death contributes to the long-term stability and health of the ecosystem.

Even in the face of human-induced disturbances, nature demonstrates a remarkable capacity for recovery. Abandoned agricultural fields, once devoid of native vegetation, gradually revert to grasslands and forests through the process of ecological succession. Pioneer species, adapted to disturbed environments, colonize the bare soil, paving the way for more complex plant communities. Over time, the ecosystem gradually rebuilds itself, regaining its complexity and biodiversity. This inherent drive towards restoration showcases nature's remarkable resilience even in the face of significant human impact.

The resilience of nature is a testament to the power of adaptation, interconnectedness, and the constant cycle of renewal. It's a reminder that even in the face of adversity, life finds a way. Observing and understanding these processes can inspire us to embrace change and to find creative solutions to our own challenges. By learning from the resilient strategies of the natural world, we can better navigate the complexities of our own lives and strive for a more sustainable future. This inherent strength, woven into the fabric of every ecosystem, offers a powerful lesson in perseverance and the enduring power of life. It reminds us that change is not always destructive, but can often be the catalyst for renewal and growth, a principle deeply embedded in the very essence of the natural world. The whispering shadows of the spectral garden hold within them a profound message of hope and resilience, a message we can all learn from.

6 Chapter 6: Conservation and the Future

The quiet symphony of the night is increasingly threatened. Human activity casts a long shadow, disrupting the delicate balance of nocturnal ecosystems. Light pollution washes out the stars, confusing migrating birds and disorienting nocturnal insects that are vital food sources for bats, nightjars, and even some owl species. Habitat loss, driven by deforestation, urbanization, and agricultural expansion, fragments the landscapes these creatures depend on, isolating populations and reducing genetic diversity. Consider the specific needs of the Long-eared Owl, a species reliant on dense, mature forests for nesting and hunting. Fragmentation can leave them vulnerable to predation and reduce their access to crucial prey. Similarly, the Heath Nightjar, which thrives in open heathland and shrubland, faces habitat loss as these areas are converted for agriculture or development. The unseen mycorrhizal networks, crucial to the health of forests and the survival of plant life that supports these nocturnal animals, are also impacted by soil compaction from heavy machinery, pesticide use, and invasive plant species.

The delicate balance of nocturnal ecosystems depends on the intricate interplay of predator and prey, intricate networks of life adapted to the dark. Owls, with their specialized hearing and silent flight, control rodent populations, playing a crucial role in maintaining forest health. Nightjars, in turn, consume vast numbers of nocturnal insects, keeping insect populations in check. The mycorrhizal networks beneath the surface connect plants, facilitating the exchange of nutrients and water, enhancing the overall resilience of the forest ecosystem. Disruptions to any part of this web can have cascading effects. For instance, the decline of moth populations due to light pollution can have a direct impact on the breeding success of nightjars that depend on them as a primary food source. Similarly, the destruction of old-growth forests, which are crucial nesting sites for owls, can lead to a decrease in owl populations, potentially leading to an increase in rodent populations. This in turn can affect the regeneration of trees and the overall health of the forest. The intricate relationships within these ecosystems highlight the importance of a holistic conservation approach.

Protecting these nocturnal ecosystems requires a multifaceted approach. Dark sky initiatives, which aim to reduce light pollution, can have a significant positive impact on nocturnal wildlife. These initiatives involve implementing measures such as using shielded lighting fixtures that direct light downwards, reducing the overall brightness of lights, and using lights with warmer color temperatures that are less disruptive to nocturnal animals. Preserving and restoring habitats is equally crucial. This involves protecting existing old-growth forests, creating corridors to connect fragmented habitats, and managing land in a way that supports the needs of nocturnal species. Consider the specific needs of the Eastern Whip-poor-will, a nightjar species that nests on the forest floor. Maintaining a mosaic of forest types, including open woodlands and areas with leaf litter, can create suitable nesting habitat.

Our role as stewards of the environment is paramount. Education and awareness play a vital role in fostering a sense of responsibility for the natural world. Supporting conservation organizations that are actively working to protect nocturnal habitats is another essential step. Individual actions, such as reducing our own light footprint and making environmentally conscious choices, can collectively make a significant difference. By understanding the specific needs of nocturnal species, we can tailor our conservation efforts to be most effective. For example, reducing pesticide use can protect the health of insect populations, which are vital food sources for many nocturnal animals. Supporting sustainable forestry practices that prioritize the preservation of old-growth trees can provide essential nesting sites for owls and other cavity-nesting species.

The future of these spectral gardens hinges on our collective actions. By recognizing the intrinsic value of nocturnal ecosystems and taking proactive steps to protect them, we can ensure that the whispering shadows and the subtle language of the night continue to enrich our world. The intricate tapestry of life that unfolds under the cover of darkness deserves our respect and protection. By working together, we can safeguard these fragile ecosystems for generations to come, preserving the symphony of shadows that plays out each night in the whispering woods. This requires not just scientific understanding but also a fundamental shift in our perception of the natural world, recognizing the interconnectedness of all living things and our place within this intricate web.

6.1   Protecting the Night

The cloak of night, often perceived as a time of vulnerability, is, in reality, a vibrant ecosystem teeming with life. Protecting this delicate balance requires understanding the specific threats that darkness faces and taking targeted action to mitigate them. Light pollution, a pervasive issue in our increasingly urbanized world, disrupts the natural rhythms of nocturnal creatures. For owls, whose hunting strategies rely on the cover of darkness, excessive artificial light can be detrimental. It washes out the starlight they use for navigation, making it harder to pinpoint prey. Similarly, nightjars, with their crepuscular habits, find their foraging disrupted, their insect prey drawn away by the allure of artificial lights. The impact goes even deeper, affecting the very foundation of the forest floor. Mycorrhizal fungi, sensitive to changes in light and temperature, can be negatively impacted by the constant illumination of urban sprawl, disrupting their symbiotic relationships with plant life and hindering nutrient exchange.

Addressing light pollution requires a multi-pronged approach. Advocating for responsible lighting practices in our communities is crucial. This includes promoting the use of low-intensity, downward-facing lights that minimize light trespass into natural areas. Supporting initiatives like "Lights Out" programs, which encourage businesses and residents to turn off non-essential

lighting during peak migration periods, can also make a significant difference. On a personal level, minimizing outdoor lighting on our properties and
opting for motion-sensor lights rather than constant illumination are small
changes with a big impact. These efforts not only protect nocturnal wildlife
but also reduce energy consumption, a win-win situation for both the environment and our wallets.

Habitat loss and fragmentation pose another significant threat to the nocturnal world. As forests are cleared for development, owls lose crucial nesting
sites and hunting grounds. Nightjars, dependent on specific vegetation types
for camouflage and nesting, find their already limited habitats shrinking.
The delicate mycorrhizal networks that underpin the health of the forest are
severed, disrupting the intricate communication and resource sharing between trees and fungi. Conserving existing habitats and restoring degraded
areas is paramount. Supporting organizations dedicated to land preservation
and habitat restoration is a vital step. Participating in local reforestation
projects and advocating for responsible land management practices within
our communities are equally important. We can also contribute by creating wildlife-friendly backyards and gardens, providing native plants, water
sources, and nesting boxes, effectively extending existing habitats into our
urban landscapes.

Pesticide use, though often aimed at controlling unwanted pests, can have
devastating consequences for nocturnal ecosystems. Owls and nightjars, as
top predators in their food webs, are particularly vulnerable to bioaccumula-
tion, the process by which toxins accumulate in their bodies as they consume

contaminated prey. This can lead to reproductive issues, weakened immune systems, and even death. Moreover, pesticides can disrupt the delicate balance of the mycorrhizal network, harming the beneficial fungi that support plant growth and forest health. Transitioning to organic gardening practices and supporting sustainable agriculture are essential for mitigating the harmful effects of pesticides. By choosing organic produce and advocating for stricter regulations on pesticide use, we can contribute to a healthier environment for nocturnal wildlife and ourselves.

Human disturbance, whether intentional or unintentional, can also disrupt the delicate balance of the night. Noise pollution from traffic, construction, and other human activities can interfere with the sensitive hearing of owls and nightjars, hindering their ability to hunt and communicate. Encroachment into natural areas can disturb nesting sites and force animals to abandon their young. Respecting the boundaries of natural areas and minimizing our impact when we do venture into them is crucial. Educating ourselves and others about the importance of minimizing noise pollution and refraining from disturbing wildlife is essential for fostering coexistence. Supporting initiatives like citizen science projects, which monitor owl and nightjar populations and provide valuable data for conservation efforts, allows us to actively participate in protecting these fascinating creatures.

By understanding the interconnectedness of the nocturnal world and the specific threats it faces, we can take targeted action to protect the night and ensure that the whispers of owls, the churring of nightjars, and the silent communication of the mycorrhizal web continue to enrich our planet for generations to come. This requires not only individual actions but also collective efforts to advocate for responsible environmental policies and support conservation initiatives that safeguard the delicate balance of life in the shadows. The preservation of these nocturnal ecosystems is not just about protecting individual species, it's about preserving the intricate web of life that supports the health and resilience of our planet as a whole.

6.2 Preserving Habitats

The preservation of nocturnal habitats is crucial for the survival of species like owls, nightjars, and the intricate mycorrhizal networks that support the entire forest ecosystem. These habitats, shrouded in darkness and often overlooked, face a unique set of threats that demand specific conservation strategies. Light pollution, for instance, disrupts the natural rhythms of nocturnal animals, impacting their hunting, mating, and navigation. Owls, reliant on darkness for their hunting prowess, can be disoriented by artificial light, making them vulnerable to collisions and reducing their hunting success. Nightjars, too, are affected, their twilight displays hampered by the intrusion of artificial illumination. Addressing this issue requires thoughtful urban planning, minimizing light trespass into natural areas, and promoting the use of low-impact lighting solutions.

Habitat fragmentation, the breaking up of continuous habitats into smaller, isolated patches, poses another significant threat. This fragmentation, often caused by human development, agriculture, and road construction, restricts the movement of nocturnal animals, limiting their access to essential resources like food, mates, and nesting sites. Owls, with their territorial nature, require large, undisturbed areas to hunt and breed. Fragmentation reduces the availability of such territories, impacting their population densities and overall health. Nightjars, with their specific habitat requirements, are also highly vulnerable to habitat loss and fragmentation. Connecting fragmented landscapes through corridors of natural vegetation is crucial for allowing these species to move freely and maintain healthy populations.

Forest management practices play a vital role in preserving these sensitive habitats. Sustainable forestry techniques, which prioritize the maintenance of old-growth forests and minimize clear-cutting, are essential for providing suitable nesting sites for owls and protecting the understory vegetation crucial for nightjar foraging. Moreover, preserving deadwood and fallen logs is essential for maintaining insect populations, a critical food source for both owls and nightjars. These decaying materials also play a crucial role in the mycorrhizal network, providing a substrate for fungal growth and promoting the healthy functioning of this vital underground network.

The use of pesticides and herbicides poses a considerable threat to the delicate balance of nocturnal ecosystems. These chemicals can directly impact insect populations, the primary food source for many nocturnal animals, including nightjars. Furthermore, these chemicals can accumulate in the food chain, impacting higher trophic levels, including owls, and disrupting the delicate balance of the ecosystem. Promoting organic farming practices and reducing the reliance on harmful chemicals is essential for protecting these sensitive species and the ecosystems they inhabit. Protecting the intricate mycorrhizal network, which plays a vital role in nutrient cycling and plant health, is also essential. Minimizing soil disturbance, avoiding compaction, and promoting diverse plant communities contribute to the health of these vital fungal networks, ultimately benefiting the entire forest ecosystem.

Preserving the natural soundscapes of nocturnal habitats is equally crucial. Noise pollution from traffic, industry, and human activities can interfere with the acoustic communication of nocturnal animals, impacting their ability to find mates, defend territories, and locate prey. Owls, with their exceptional hearing, are particularly sensitive to noise pollution. Nightjars, whose churring calls are an integral part of their mating rituals, are also vulnerable to acoustic disruption. Creating buffer zones around sensitive habitats and implementing noise reduction measures can help mitigate the impacts of noise pollution. The intricate web of life within nocturnal ecosystems is often hidden from view, but its importance is undeniable. By understanding the specific threats facing these habitats and implementing targeted conservation strategies, we can safeguard the future of owls, nightjars, the mycorrhizal network, and the entire symphony of life that unfolds under the cover of darkness. Our role as stewards of the environment is to ensure that these whispering shadows continue to echo through the spectral garden for generations to come. Protecting the night is not just about preserving darkness; it's about protecting the intricate web of life that thrives within it, recognizing the vital role that these often-overlooked ecosystems play in the overall health of our planet.

6.3 Our Role as Stewards

We stand at a critical juncture. The whispers of the spectral garden are growing fainter, masked by the encroaching sounds of human activity. The owls' hunting grounds shrink, fragmented by development. The nightjars' twilight chorus is drowned out by artificial lights. The delicate mycorrhizal web, the very foundation of the forest, is disrupted by pollution and habitat loss. Our actions, both large and small, reverberate through this interconnected ecosystem, impacting the delicate balance that has evolved over millennia. We have a profound responsibility, a moral imperative, to act as stewards for this fragile world.

Stewardship is not simply a passive appreciation of nature. It demands active participation, a commitment to understanding and protecting the intricate web of life. It requires us to recognize that we are not separate from nature, but an integral part of it. Our well-being is inextricably linked to the health of the ecosystems we inhabit. When we harm the forest, we ultimately harm ourselves. Protecting the spectral garden is not just an act of altruism; it is an act of self-preservation.

Consider the owls, silent hunters of the night. Their declining numbers reflect the degradation of their habitats, the loss of old-growth forests, and the decrease in prey populations. To protect the owls, we must advocate for responsible forest management practices, reduce the use of harmful pesticides, and preserve the natural corridors they rely on for hunting and nesting. This requires supporting organizations dedicated to owl conservation and educating others about the importance of these magnificent birds.

The nightjars, with their ethereal churrs, face similar challenges. Light pollution disrupts their nocturnal navigation and foraging behaviors, making them vulnerable to predators and reducing their breeding success. We can mitigate this by minimizing outdoor lighting, using low-intensity bulbs, and advocating for dark sky initiatives in our communities. By creating a more natural nightscape, we can help protect these elusive birds and the other nocturnal creatures that depend on darkness for survival.

Beneath the surface, the mycorrhizal web, a hidden network of fungal filaments, plays a crucial role in forest health. This intricate web connects trees and other plants, allowing them to communicate and share resources. However, soil compaction, chemical pollution, and invasive species can disrupt this delicate network, weakening the entire forest ecosystem. Sustainable land management practices, such as reducing tillage and promoting diverse plant communities, are essential for preserving the health of the mycorrhizal web and the forest it supports.

Our role as stewards extends beyond simply protecting individual species. It encompasses a broader understanding of the interconnectedness of the ecosystem. We must recognize that the health of the forest depends on the health of all its components, from the smallest microbe to the largest predator. By promoting biodiversity, restoring degraded habitats, and reducing our environmental footprint, we can help ensure the long-term health and resilience of the spectral garden.

This stewardship requires constant vigilance, a willingness to learn, and a commitment to action. It demands that we educate ourselves about the complex ecological relationships within the forest and the threats they face. It necessitates that we engage in citizen science initiatives, monitoring populations, and reporting observations to researchers. It requires us to support policies that protect natural habitats and promote sustainable land management practices.

Finally, it compels us to share our knowledge and passion with others. By inspiring others to appreciate the beauty and importance of the spectral garden, we can create a collective movement for its protection. We can foster a sense of wonder and respect for the intricate web of life that connects us all. The whispers of the spectral garden are calling to us, urging us to embrace our role as stewards. The future of this precious ecosystem, and indeed our own future, depends on our willingness to listen and act. Let us answer that call with courage, dedication, and a deep commitment to preserving the wonders of the natural world. The time for action is now, before the whispers fade into silence. Our legacy as stewards will be determined by the choices we make today.

7 Epilogue: A Symphony of Shadows

The spectral garden breathes. Not with the rustle of leaves in a summer breeze, but with the hushed, rhythmic pulse of life unseen. Beneath the moon's pale gaze, a silent choreography unfolds. The owl, a feathered phantom, glides through the silvered branches, its keen eyes reflecting the starlight. A nightjar, cloaked in the shadows, calls out its eerie churring serenade, a melody woven into the tapestry of night. Below the surface, the mycorrhizal web hums with a silent exchange, a subterranean language of nutrients and signals passing between the roots of trees, a hidden conversation that sustains the forest's lifeblood. This is a world of whispers and shadows, a symphony played in muted tones, yet brimming with vibrant life. We have journeyed deep into this hidden realm, explored the lives of owls and nightjars, unravelled the secrets of the fungal network, and learned to listen to the subtle language of the forest. We have witnessed the delicate dance between predator and prey, the ceaseless cycle of life and death that plays out under the veil of night. We have come to understand that the shadows are not a void, but a vibrant ecosystem teeming with life, each organism playing its vital role in maintaining the delicate balance of nature. Consider the owl, a silent hunter with eyes that pierce the darkness. Its presence is a testament to the intricate web of life, a predator that shapes the populations of its prey, influencing the very structure of the forest. Reflect on the nightjar, a master of camouflage, its churring call a haunting echo in the twilight. Its existence highlights the remarkable adaptations that allow creatures to thrive in the most challenging environments, exploiting niches unseen by the diurnal eye. Remember the mycorrhizal network, the hidden hand that nourishes the forest, connecting trees in a silent embrace. This intricate web demonstrates the power of symbiosis, the interconnectedness of life beneath the surface.

The spectral garden is not merely a collection of individual organisms, but a complex, interconnected system where each element plays a vital role. The owl, the nightjar, the mycorrhizal web, and countless other unseen actors participate in a continuous exchange of energy and information, a symphony of interactions that creates the vibrant tapestry of life. The rustling of leaves, the hooting of an owl, the chirping of crickets, the silent growth of fungi beneath the soil – these are all instruments in this grand orchestral performance.

As we emerge from the spectral garden, let us carry with us a renewed sense of wonder and appreciation for the hidden world that surrounds us. Let us remember that the shadows are not empty spaces, but vibrant ecosystems teeming with life. Let the lessons of the nocturnal world – the importance of balance, interconnectedness, and resilience – guide our actions as stewards of this planet.

We have a responsibility to protect these delicate ecosystems, to ensure that the symphony of shadows continues to play on. By preserving habitats, reducing light pollution, and promoting sustainable practices, we can contribute to the health and vitality of the spectral garden. The future of these nocturnal wonders depends on our understanding and our commitment to their preservation.

The spectral garden is a reminder that the world is full of mysteries, wonders yet to be discovered, and stories yet to be told. It beckons us to explore, to listen, to observe, and to appreciate the intricate beauty of the natural world. It is a testament to the resilience of life, the power of adaptation, and the enduring magic of the night.

Let us not forget the lessons whispered by the shadows. The interconnectedness of all living things, the delicate balance of nature, and the importance of preserving these fragile ecosystems. As we step back into the light, let us carry with us the echoes of the spectral garden, a constant reminder of the hidden symphony of life that unfolds under the cover of darkness. May this understanding inspire us to act as guardians of the night, protecting the delicate web of life for generations to come.

The spectral garden is a place of constant renewal, a testament to the enduring power of nature. The cycle of life and death continues, the whispers of the forest echo through the night, and the symphony of shadows plays on, a testament to the intricate beauty and enduring magic of the natural world.

www.ingramcontent.com/pod-product-compliance
Ingram Content Group UK Ltd.
Pitfield, Milton Keynes, MK11 3LW, UK
UKHW021437240125
4283UKWH00041B/641